Blender

Blender

Perfect sauces, soups, purées and smoothies

Linda Doeser

MARKS&
SPENCER

Marks and Spencer p.l.c.
PO Box 3339, Chester CH99 9QS
www.marksandspencer.com

Copyright © Exclusive Editions 2005

ISBN: 1-84461-326-7

Printed in China

Author: Linda Doeser
Editor: Fiona Biggs
Designed by Fiona Roberts
Photography: Karen Thomas
Home Economist: Annie Nichols

Notes for the Reader

This book uses both metric and imperial measurements. Follow the same units of
measurement throughout; do not mix metric and imperial. All spoon measurements are
level; teaspoons are assumed to be 5 ml and tablespoons are assumed to be 15 ml.
Unless otherwise stated, milk is assumed to be full fat, individual vegetables such as
potatoes are medium, and pepper is freshly ground black pepper. Recipes using raw or
very lightly cooked eggs should be avoided by infants, the elderly, pregnant women,
convalescents and anyone suffering from an illness. The times given are an approximate
guide only. Preparation times differ according to the techniques used by different people
and the cooking times may also vary from those given. Optional ingredients, variations or
serving suggestions have not been included in the calculations.

Contents

INTRODUCTION

A blender is not only one of the most useful appliances to have in the kitchen but also one of the most common. Yet, strangely, it is often under-used. Most people have their own standard recipes for which they invariably get the blender out of the cupboard.

A mum with a young baby might use it for puréeing tiny portions of family dishes, a keen gardener might make batches of soup for the freezer when there is a glut of vegetables and an enthusiastic hostess might press it into service for dips, pâtés and terrines. Yet the rest of the time, it is frequently overlooked and unused.

This is a shame as the blender really is the cook's friend and can take care of all sorts of tedious and time-consuming tasks effortlessly and quickly. It's rather like having your very own assistant chef. For example, think how often recipes call for breadcrumbs, whether for home-made burgers or stuffing for the Christmas turkey. Why make your arm ache and risk grazing your fingers on a grater, when you can produce them quickly and painlessly in the blender? Recipes frequently specify chopped or even finely chopped herbs. Save time and effort by doing this in the blender. It's also great for making smoothies and milkshakes, fruit drinks and wonderfully frothy hot chocolate.

In the recipes in this book the blender plays a more central role, although, of course, it can still be used for the initial preparation of ingredients, such as chopping nuts. The recipes amply demonstrate what a labour-saving device this clever appliance is and will, it is hoped, inspire you to

new culinary heights. Take something as simple and popular as mayonnaise, for example. Of course, there are many commercial varieties available but these often contain flavourings and other additives and tend to be unappetizingly gelatinous in texture. Moreover, 'real' mayonnaise tastes so much better. However, it is an incredible bore to make by hand and the temptation to try to speed up the process, in spite of the fact that this results in curdled egg yolk, is almost irresistible. Making it in the blender will spare your aching wrist and also allows you to achieve the precise consistency that suits you. As a bonus, the basic recipe (see page 28) also includes two other mayonnaise-based sauces.

Types of blender

There are basically two types of blender – goblet and hand-held. The recipes in this book are designed for a goblet blender, sometimes also known as a liquidizer.

Goblet blender: This consists of a base in which the motor is located and a removable tall cylindrical bowl, or goblet, with a lid. It may be a single, free-standing appliance or part of a combination with a food processor or electric mixer. The goblet is usually made of transparent plastic or glass and varies in capacity from about 600 ml/1 pint to 1.5 litres/2¾ pints. Many have a handle and a pouring lip and they usually have a hole in the lid through which ingredients can be added while the motor is

running – this is essential for some recipes, such as Hollandaise Sauce (see page 38). A graduated scale on the side of the goblet makes measuring liquids very simple and most blender goblets also have a line designating the maximum capacity that the blender can safely cope with at any one time.

There are four small, extremely sharp blades located in the base of the goblet at right angles to each other. As these rotate the centre of the mixture forms a well and the mixture is pushed up the sides of the goblet and then falls back down onto the blades. Unlike in food processors, the blades are not usually removable.

The blender, once plugged in, is operated by an on/off switch and may also have a switch or dial that allows you to vary the speed. Some models also have a pulse mode. As most blending needs to take place at high speed, a single-speed appliance should not present much problem. Lower speeds are generally used only for chopping. The blender will continue to run until you switch it off, although the manufacturer usually includes a safety cut-out. Nowadays, blenders are made so that they will not switch on until the lid is properly fitted. When they were first introduced in the 1950s, this was not always the case and people sometimes had unfortunate accidents when the contents of the blender were sprayed all over the kitchen or, far worse, they were badly injured by foolishly inserting their fingers while the motor was still running.

Hand-held blender: This has a handle and a wand at the base of which is a rotating blade. The motor is located in the handle which also incorporates the switch. It has a single speed and works for as long as the control switch, also on the handle, is depressed or in the on position. This is an in-built safety feature. Some models have extra attachments, such as a whisk, and interchangeable blades. This type of blender is useful for blending small quantities, particularly when they are still in a saucepan. It cannot be used for all the recipes in this book, but works well for some sauces, soups and drinks, for example. It is not usually suitable for blending dry ingredients.

Choosing a blender

The cost of blenders can vary considerably, so if you're not going to be using one frequently, it is sensible to avoid the more expensive and sophisticated models. If you are a very enthusiastic cook a combined blender and mixer or blender and food processor might be the best choice, but remember that this will take up a lot of space. The size of your family is also a consideration. If you will be preparing only small quantities, a large goblet is more trouble than it's worth as the food tends to get lost inside it. A mum with a baby might find a medium-size goblet blender is ideal for adult foods, while an inexpensive hand-held blender is more appropriate for preparing baby purées.

Using a goblet blender

As with all electrical appliances, it is important to read the manufacturer's instructions. These will always include information about safe running times and maximum capacity, as well as advice about the kinds of foods that are suitable for processing in a blender and the care and maintenance of your particular model.

Make sure that the blender is standing securely on a flat surface and that the electrical cord is not overhanging. Fit the goblet into position. Blenders work best with relatively small quantities of ingredients, so it is often better to process in two or more batches. This is particularly important if you are using the blender to chop dry ingredients, such as vegetables. Never fill the blender with more than the specified maximum capacity and, in the case of liquid, which is inclined to froth up, it should not be more than one-third to one-half full. Never leave the blender switched on and unattended and make sure that it is out of the reach of children.

Batters: Blend the egg, milk and any other liquids to combine them, then, with the motor running, gradually add the dry ingredients through the hole in the lid.

Chopping: Cut vegetables, fruit, cheese, chocolate, chicken, etc. into fairly small pieces of about the same size. Remove stones and bones and process in small batches at maximum speed. Tip the first batch into a bowl before adding the next. If you are chopping candied peel, cut it into fairly small pieces then process in small batches with a little sugar to prevent it from sticking.

Cooked foods and leftovers: These are best processed with the addition of a little stock, water, gravy, fruit juice, wine or other liquid that is appropriate to the flavour. Cut large pieces into smaller, even-sized pieces before adding them to the blender and process in small batches. If you are processing stews, casseroles and soups, make sure that you include liquid with the solid ingredients.

Breadcrumbs: Tear slices of bread into small pieces and break up biscuits. With the motor running, drop these into the blender through the hole in the lid. Process in small batches. For dry breadcrumbs, use day-old bread and dry it in a preheated oven, 120°C/250°F/Gas Mark $1/2$, for 20–25 minutes before breaking it into pieces and processing in the blender.

Nuts: These should be processed in small batches at low speed. Turn the blender on and off during processing for maximum fineness.

Herbs: Strip the leaves from the stems and, with the motor running, drop them into the blender through the hole in the lid. They can be coarsely or finely chopped.

Ice cubes: Blenders are not usually robust enough to cope with whole ice cubes. Use cracked ice when making slushes and other drinks (see page 73).

Purées: When making terrines, pâtés and baby foods, chop the ingredients into fairly small pieces before processing in small batches. Dips can usually be processed in larger quantities. When processing cooked vegetables and fruit, such as boiled carrots and stewed apples, and raw soft vegetables and fruit, such as avocados and raspberries, fill the goblet no more than one-third full. Extra liquid is not required. Process on high speed and scrape down the sides occasionally. To get rid of seeds, press the purée through a nylon sieve.

Soups: Leave to cool slightly before pouring into the blender. Err on the side of caution and do not fill more than half full. Hold the lid firmly before switching on.

Note: Do not grind coffee beans or spices in a blender.

Using a hand-held blender

This is a convenient way to purée small quantities of food and to blend sauces and soups in the saucepan. Read the manufacturer's instructions for guidance on your model. Many are not suitable for chopping dry ingredients, for example. Put the wand into the pan or bowl – don't immerse the handle – and switch on, then move the wand smoothly through the ingredients in a figure-of-eight. Small quantities of splashy ingredients, such as batters, are best blended in a jug. A hand-held blender can be used for processing creamy dips, most soups, eggs for omelettes and scrambled egg, many sauces, soft fruits and butter icing. It is also suitable for beating ice cream and sorbets during freezing and for preparing cheesecake fillings.

Hints and tips

◎ When chopping ingredients in the blender, process in small batches. If there is too much in the blender, part will be finely chopped, while the rest will be in larger pieces.

◎ To avoid ingredients sticking, make sure there is sufficient liquid and that the blender is not too full. When processing thick mixtures scrape down the sides of the goblet with a spatula from time to time.

◎ Always use plastic utensils when scraping down the sides of the goblet and spooning a mixture out of it to avoid scratching the sides. For the same reason, don't clean the goblet with scouring pads or abrasives.

◎ If liquid leaks out of the top of the blender, switch off, mop up and remove some of the liquid. Soups and drinks tend to froth up, so never more than half-fill the goblet.

◎ Lumpy sauces, soups and purées need longer processing. If you're worried about the motor overheating, stop and let it cool for a few minutes before continuing.

◎ Keep an eye on what you're doing to avoid over-processing. If you are chopping dried fruit in a blender without paying attention, you'll end up with a purée.

◎ If the motor cuts out during use, switch off, wait for 15–20 minutes for the motor to cool, then try again. If the blender still won't work, check the fuse.

Care of the blender

Switch off and unplug the blender before washing it. Check the manufacturer's instructions for dishwasher safety. Otherwise, wash the goblet in warm, soapy water. Rinse and dry thoroughly. Remember that the blades are very sharp. Stubborn stains can usually be removed with a little vegetable oil. If food is trapped in the blades, pour a little soapy water into the goblet, fit it back in the base unit and switch on briefly. Rinse and dry thoroughly. Never immerse the base in water. Simply wipe with a damp cloth and then dry. Switch off a hand-held blender and remove the wand. Wash in warm, soapy water, rinse and dry. If the wand is not detachable, wash the blades with warm soapy water without getting the handle wet. Rinse and dry.

CHAPTER 1: SOUPS

Gazpacho

This is probably the world's best-known chilled soup. It's so tasty and colourful it certainly deserves its reputation.

Serves 6

Preparation time: 30 minutes, plus 2 hours' chilling

Cooking time: 2–3 minutes

Ingredients

250 g/9 oz white bread slices, crusts removed

700 g/1 lb 9 oz tomatoes, peeled and chopped

3 garlic cloves, coarsely chopped

2 red peppers, deseeded and coarsely chopped

1 cucumber, peeled, deseeded and chopped

5 tbsp extra virgin olive oil

5 tbsp red wine vinegar

1 tbsp tomato purée

850 ml/1 $\frac{1}{2}$ pints water

salt and pepper

To garnish

2 tbsp olive oil

1 garlic clove, finely chopped

4 slices white bread, crusts removed and cut into 5-mm/$\frac{1}{4}$-in cubes

6 spring onions, thinly sliced

$\frac{1}{4}$ cucumber, diced

1 Tear the bread into pieces and place in the blender. Process briefly to make breadcrumbs and transfer to a large bowl. Add the tomatoes, garlic, red peppers, cucumber, oil, vinegar and tomato purée. Mix well.

2 Working in batches, place the tomato mixture with about the same amount of the measured water in the blender and process to a purée. Transfer to another bowl. When all the tomato mixture and water have been blended together, stir well and season to taste with salt and pepper. Cover with clingfilm and chill in the refrigerator for at least 2 hours, but no longer than 12 hours.

3 Heat the oil in a heavy-based frying pan. Add the garlic and the bread cubes and cook over a medium heat, stirring and tossing frequently, for 2–3 minutes until golden brown. Remove from the pan with a slotted spoon and drain on kitchen paper.

4 Arrange the garnishes on separate small dishes and serve with the soup.

Cook's tip
Other traditional garnishes for gazpacho include deseeded and finely diced red and green peppers and chopped hard-boiled egg.

CHILLED AVOCADO SOUP

This delicate soup is made entirely in the blender and is perfect for an al fresco meal. Serve within 2 hours of making to avoid discoloration.

Serves 4
Preparation time: 10 minutes, plus 30 minutes' chilling
Cooking time: 0 minutes

Ingredients

1 tbsp lemon juice
2 avocados
1 tbsp snipped fresh chives, plus extra to garnish
1 tbsp chopped fresh flat-leaf parsley
425 ml/15 fl oz cold chicken stock

300 ml/10 fl oz single cream, plus
  extra to garnish
dash of Worcestershire sauce
salt and pepper

1 Put the lemon juice into the blender. Halve the avocados and remove the stones. Scoop out the flesh and chop coarsely.

2 Place the avocado flesh, chives, parsley, stock, cream and Worcestershire sauce in the blender and process to a smooth purée.

3 Transfer to a bowl and season to taste with salt and pepper. Cover the bowl tightly with clingfilm and chill in the refrigerator for at least 30 minutes. To serve, stir, then ladle into chilled soup bowls and garnish with a swirl of cream and a sprinkling of snipped chives.

Cook's tip
Avocado flesh turns an unappealing brownish colour when exposed to the air. It is important to put the lemon juice into the blender before you add the avocado to help prevent this. It is also important that the soup is tightly covered while chilling.

Variation
For a vegetarian version of this soup, substitute vegetable stock for the chicken stock. If you like, you can use natural yogurt instead of single cream.

Tomato Soup

Once you have tasted home-made tomato soup you'll never want to buy the canned version again.

 Serves 4

 Preparation time: 15 minutes

 Cooking time: 25 minutes

Ingredients

55 g/2 oz butter

1 small onion, finely chopped

450 g/1 lb tomatoes, coarsely chopped

1 bay leaf

3 tbsp plain flour

600 ml/1 pint milk

salt and pepper

2 tbsp torn fresh basil leaves, to garnish

1 Melt half the butter in a saucepan. Add the onion and cook over a low heat, stirring occasionally, for 5–6 minutes until softened. Add the tomatoes and bay leaf and cook, stirring occasionally, for 15 minutes, or until pulpy.

2 Meanwhile, melt the remaining butter in another saucepan. Add the flour and cook, stirring constantly, for 1 minute. Remove the pan from the heat and gradually stir in the milk. Return to the heat, season with salt and pepper and bring to the boil, stirring constantly. Continue to cook, stirring, until smooth and thickened. Transfer to the top of a double boiler.

3 When the tomatoes are pulpy, remove the pan from the heat. Discard the bay leaf and pour the tomato mixture into the blender. Process until smooth, then push through a sieve into a clean saucepan. Bring the tomato purée to the boil, then gradually stir it into the milk mixture. Season to taste with salt and pepper. Ladle into warm bowls, garnish with basil leaves and serve immediately.

Cook's tip
It is essential that the tomatoes are really ripe for maximum flavour and sweetness. Ideally, use home-grown, sun-ripened tomatoes or vine tomatoes. If these are not available, you may need to add 1–2 teaspoons sugar to sweeten the purée.

Variation
Add 85 g/3 oz diced lean bacon with the onion in step 1 and garnish the soup with 2 tablespoons chopped fresh parsley instead of basil.

CREAMY CARROT SOUP

With its attractive colour and sweet, rich flavour, this easy soup is always popular with all the family.

Serves 4
Preparation time: 20 minutes
Cooking time: 25 minutes

Ingredients

55 g/2 oz butter
1 onion, finely chopped
1 leek, finely chopped
450 g/1 lb carrots, grated
1 tbsp plain flour

1.2 litres/2 pints hot chicken or
    vegetable stock
150 ml/5 fl oz double cream
salt and pepper
fresh basil leaves, to garnish (optional)

1 Melt the butter in a large, heavy-based saucepan. Add the onion and leek and cook, stirring occasionally, for 5–6 minutes until softened. Stir in the carrots, lower the heat, cover and cook for 5 minutes.

2 Sprinkle in the flour and cook, stirring, for 1 minute. Gradually stir in the hot stock. Bring to the boil, then simmer for 8 minutes.

3 Remove the pan from the heat and leave the soup to cool slightly. Pour it into the blender and process to a purée. Transfer to a clean saucepan and bring back to a simmer. Stir in the cream and simmer for a further 2 minutes. Season to taste, ladle into warm bowls and serve, garnished with basil leaves, if desired.

Cook's tip
You can use the blender to chop the onion, leek and carrots into small dice. Chop them coarsely first, then process in small batches at maximum speed.

THAI PORK & PRAWN SOUP

*Soup is almost always served as part of a Thai meal and is often eaten
as a snack, so recipes are many, varied and utterly delicious.*

🍽 Serves 6

🥣 Preparation time: 20 minutes

🧤 Cooking time: 1 hour 10 minutes

Ingredients

175 g/6 oz pork fillet, cut into very thin strips

85 g/3 oz Thai jasmine rice

1.4 litres/2½ pints chicken stock

425 ml/15 fl oz coconut milk

3 tbsp lime juice

1 tbsp Thai fish sauce

2 garlic cloves, chopped

1 lemon grass stalk, finely chopped

2 kaffir lime leaves

1 fresh green chilli, deseeded and chopped

2 tbsp chopped fresh coriander

300 g/10½ oz cooked, peeled prawns

fresh coriander sprigs, sliced into julienne strips,
   to garnish

1 Put the pork, rice, stock, coconut milk, lime juice, fish sauce, garlic, lemon grass, kaffir lime leaves, chilli and half the coriander into a large saucepan and bring to the boil over a medium heat. Lower the heat, cover and simmer, stirring occasionally, for 1 hour.

2 Remove from the heat and leave to cool slightly. Remove and discard the kaffir lime leaves, then transfer to the blender and process to a smooth purée.

3 Transfer the soup to a clean saucepan and bring to the boil. Add the prawns and cook for 2–3 minutes more until heated through. Ladle into warm bowls, garnish with coriander strips and serve.

Cook's tip

*Thai jasmine rice, sometimes called fragrant rice, Thai
fish sauce, canned coconut milk, lemon grass and kaffir
lime leaves are available from most supermarkets and
specialist Asian food stores.*

Variation

*For a more substantial soup, add 225 g/8 oz drained
canned straw mushrooms with the prawns in step 3.
Alternatively, substitute 450 g/1 lb peeled raw tiger
prawns for the cooked prawns. Add them in step 3 and
simmer for 5 minutes, or until they turn pink.*

PRAWN BISQUE

A bisque is a thick, creamy fish soup based on a shellfish purée and has a long and venerable history.

Serves 4
Preparation time: 30 minutes
Cooking time: 45–50 minutes

Ingredients

450 g/1 lb raw prawns	4 tbsp fresh white breadcrumbs
1 tbsp sunflower oil	40 g/1 1/2 oz butter
2 shallots, sliced	pinch of freshly grated nutmeg
1 celery stick, sliced (reserve leaves for garnish)	150 ml/5 fl oz dry white wine
1 carrot, sliced	1 large egg yolk
2 tsp lemon juice	150 ml/5 fl oz double cream
1 tbsp tomato purée	salt and pepper

1 Pull off the heads and peel the prawns, reserving the heads and shells. Place the prawns in a dish, cover with clingfilm and store in the refrigerator until required.

2 Heat the oil in a large saucepan. Add the prawn heads and shells and cook over a high heat, stirring frequently, for 3–5 minutes. Lower the heat and add the shallots, celery and carrot and cook, stirring occasionally, for 5–6 minutes. Pour in 1.2 litres/2 pints water and add 1 teaspoon of the lemon juice and the tomato purée. Bring to the boil, lower the heat, cover and simmer for 25 minutes.

3 Remove the stock from the heat and strain into a bowl. Discard the contents of the strainer. Place the breadcrumbs in another bowl and add 425 ml/15 fl oz of the stock while it is still hot, then set aside.

4 Melt 25 g/1 oz of the butter in a saucepan and add the prawns. Cook, stirring and tossing constantly for 5 minutes. Add the nutmeg, remaining lemon juice and the breadcrumb and stock mixture and cook gently, stirring occasionally, for a further 5 minutes. Beat in the remaining butter.

5 Remove the mixture from the heat and transfer to the blender. Process to a smooth purée, transfer to a clean saucepan and set over a medium heat. Add the wine and remaining stock and bring to the boil.

6 Remove the pan from the heat and season with salt and pepper. Mix the egg yolk and cream in a small bowl, then stir the mixture into the soup. Return to a very low heat and cook for 1–2 minutes, but do not allow the soup to boil. Serve immediately, garnished with celery leaves.

CHICKEN SOUP

*This creamy soup is the ultimate in comfort food, although
it is also special enough to serve to guests.*

 Serves 6

 Preparation time: 20 minutes, plus cooling

 Cooking time: 1¼ hours

Ingredients

1.3 kg/3 lb chicken

1 bunch of fresh parsley

1 bay leaf

½ tsp freshly grated nutmeg

15 g/½ oz butter

2 tbsp plain flour

3 tbsp double cream

salt and pepper

1 Place the chicken in a large saucepan and add the parsley, bay leaf and nutmeg and season well with
salt. Pour in 1.4 litres/2½ pints water and bring to the boil, skimming off any scum that rises to the
surface. Lower the heat, cover and simmer gently for 1 hour.

2 Remove the pan from the heat and transfer the chicken to a chopping board. Strain the stock into a
bowl and set aside to cool. Remove and discard the skin and bones from the chicken. Cut the flesh into
small pieces.

3 Skim the fat from the top of the cooled stock, then place the stock and chicken in the blender. Process
to a smooth purée. You may need to do this in batches. Transfer the soup to a clean saucepan.

4 Make a beurre manié by blending together the butter and flour with a fork until a smooth paste forms.
Bring the soup just to boiling point, then whisk in the beurre manié in small pieces at a time. Bring to
the boil, stirring constantly, then lower the heat and simmer for 10 minutes. Stir in the cream and season
to taste with salt and pepper. Ladle into warm bowls, sprinkle with freshly ground black pepper and
serve immediately.

Cook's tip

*To speed up the cooling process, place the bowl
containing the stock in another bowl of ice cubes
or in a sink of very cold water. It is easiest to remove
the fat once it has congealed on the surface.*

Variation

*For an even more flavourful soup, substitute chicken or
vegetable stock for the water in step 1.*

CHAPTER 2: SAUCES

MAYONNAISE

This wonderfully versatile sauce is used for salad dressings and sandwich fillings and many different extra flavourings can be added.

Serves 4
Preparation time: 5 minutes
Cooking time: 0 minutes

Ingredients

Basic Mayonnaise

2 large egg yolks

1 tbsp lemon juice or white
  wine vinegar

1/4 tsp mustard powder

150 ml/5 fl oz sunflower oil

150 ml/5 fl oz extra virgin
  olive oil

salt and pepper

Rémoulade Sauce

2 eggs, hard-boiled, cooled

and shelled

1 egg yolk

1 tbsp lemon juice or white
  wine vinegar

1 1/2 tsp Dijon mustard

150 ml/5 fl oz sunflower oil

150 ml/5 fl oz extra virgin
  olive oil

2 tbsp chopped, mixed, fresh
  parsley, chives and chervil

2 gherkins, drained and very
  finely chopped

1 tbsp bottled capers, drained

salt and pepper

Garlic Mayonnaise

2 large egg yolks

1 tbsp lemon juice or white
  wine vinegar

5–6 garlic cloves, crushed

150 ml/5 fl oz sunflower oil

150 ml/5 fl oz extra virgin
  olive oil

salt and pepper

1 To make **Basic Mayonnaise**, put the egg yolks, lemon juice and mustard powder into the blender and season with a little salt and pepper. Process on medium speed for 5 seconds. With the motor running, gradually pour in both the oils through the opening in the lid. Continue processing for 1 minute, or until all the oil has been incorporated. If necessary, stop the blender and scrape down the sides with a spatula.

2 To make **Rémoulade Sauce**, rub the hard-boiled egg yolks through a sieve into the blender. (You won't need the whites.) Add the raw yolk and process briefly to mix. Add the lemon juice and mustard and season with a little salt and pepper. Process on medium speed for 5 seconds. With the motor running, gradually pour in both the oils through the opening in the lid. Continue processing for 1 minute, or until all the oil has been incorporated. Put the mayonnaise into a bowl and stir in the herbs, gherkins and capers. Serve with cold meat, fish and shellfish and grated celeriac.

3 To make **Garlic Mayonnaise**, put the egg yolks, lemon juice and garlic into the blender and season with a little salt and pepper. Process on medium speed for 5 seconds. With the motor running, gradually pour in both the oils through the opening in the lid. Continue processing for 1 minute until all the oil has been incorporated.

ROUILLE

Traditionally served with bouillabaisse and other fish dishes, this spicy red pepper sauce is usually presented separately or spread on croutons.

Makes about 175 ml/6 fl oz
Preparation time: 15 minutes
Cooking time: 5–10 minutes

Ingredients

40 g/1 ½ oz fresh white breadcrumbs
2 red peppers, halved and deseeded
1 fresh red chilli, deseeded and coarsely chopped

3 garlic cloves, coarsely chopped
125 ml/4 fl oz extra virgin olive oil
salt and pepper

1 Place the breadcrumbs in a bowl and add water to cover, then set aside. Meanwhile, put the pepper halves, skin side up, on a baking sheet and place under a preheated grill. Cook for 5–10 minutes until the skins are blistered and charred. Remove the pepper halves with tongs, place in a plastic bag and tie the top. Leave to cool.

2 When the peppers are cool enough to handle, peel off their skins, coarsely chop the flesh and place in the blender. Squeeze the excess water from the breadcrumbs and add to the blender with the chilli and garlic. Season with salt and pepper.

3 Process to a smooth paste. With the motor running, gradually add the oil through the hole in the lid until it is fully incorporated. Stop and scrape down the sides of the blender as necessary. Transfer to a bowl, cover with clingfilm and store in the refrigerator until required.

Variation

For a lighter texture, omit the breadcrumbs and add 1 egg yolk to the blender in step 2. You will probably need to add about 3 tablespoons extra olive oil in step 3. For saffron rouille, process 3 coarsely chopped garlic cloves,

1 deseeded and chopped fresh red chilli, 2 egg yolks, a large pinch of saffron threads and some salt and pepper in the blender. Then, with the motor running, add 225 ml/8 fl oz extra virgin olive oil through the hole in the lid.

PESTO

Traditionally, pesto is made by hand, uses only basil and is never served with anything other than pasta. These speedy versions, however, offer several choices.

🍽 Makes about 225 ml/8 fl oz

🥣 Preparation time: 5 minutes

🍳 Cooking time: 30–60 seconds (Sun-Dried Tomato Pesto)

Ingredients

Pesto Genovese	Sun-Dried Tomato Pesto	Tarragon Pesto
2 garlic cloves, coarsely chopped	25 g/1 oz pine nuts	2 garlic cloves, coarsely chopped
25 g/1 oz pine nuts	2 garlic cloves, coarsely chopped	25 g/1 oz blanched almonds, coarsely chopped
40 g/1½ oz fresh basil leaves	225 g/8 oz sun-dried tomatoes in oil, drained and coarsely chopped	40 g/1½ oz fresh tarragon leaves
1 tsp coarse salt	1 tsp coarse salt	1 tsp coarse salt
25 g/1 oz freshly grated Parmesan cheese	25 g/1 oz freshly grated Parmesan cheese	25 g/1 oz freshly grated Parmesan cheese
125–150 ml/4–5 fl oz extra virgin olive oil	125–150 ml/4–5 fl oz extra virgin olive oil	125–150 ml/4–5 fl oz extra virgin olive oil

1 For the **Pesto Genovese**, put the garlic, pine nuts, basil leaves and salt into the blender and process to a purée. Add the Parmesan and process briefly again. Then add 125 ml/4 fl oz oil and process again. If the consistency is too thick, add the remaining oil and process again until smooth.

2 For the **Sun-Dried Tomato Pesto**, dry-fry the pine nuts in a heavy-based frying pan for 30–60 seconds until golden. Remove from the pan and leave to cool, then place in the blender with the garlic, sun-dried tomatoes and salt. Process to a purée. Add the Parmesan and process briefly again. Then add 125 ml/4 fl oz oil and process again. If the consistency is too thick, add the remaining oil and process again until smooth.

Cook's tip
Pesto can be used to liven up many dishes. Simply coat pieces of fish and chicken or pork or lamb chops with the sauce, then bake or grill as you normally would.

Variation
You can ring the changes on the Basic Pesto Genovese with many different ingredients. Try substituting parsley for the basil and walnuts for the pine nuts or use half parsley and half rocket.

3 For the **Tarragon Pesto**, put the garlic, almonds, tarragon leaves and salt into the blender and process to a purée. Add the Parmesan and process briefly again. Then add 125 ml/4 fl oz oil and process again. If the consistency is too thick, add the remaining oil and process again until smooth.

TAPENADE

This Provençal black olive paste is great simply stirred into freshly cooked pasta and is also delicious just served with toasted bread.

 Makes about 175 ml/6 fl oz
Preparation time: 10 minutes
Cooking time: 0 minutes

Ingredients

100 g/3½ oz canned anchovy fillets

350 g/12 oz black olives, stoned and
   coarsely chopped

2 garlic cloves, coarsely chopped

2 tbsp capers, drained and rinsed

1 tbsp Dijon mustard

3 tbsp extra virgin olive oil

2 tbsp lemon juice

1 Drain the anchovies, reserving the oil from the can. Coarsely chop the fish and place in the blender. Add the reserved oil and all the remaining ingredients. Process to a smooth purée. Stop and scrape down the sides if necessary.

2 Transfer the tapenade to a dish, cover with clingfilm and chill in the refrigerator until required. If you are not planning to use the tapenade until the following day (or even the one after), cover the surface with a layer of olive oil to prevent it from drying out.

Cook's tip
This is quite a salty combination, so you may prefer to de-salt the anchovies first. Place them in a shallow dish, pour in enough cold water or milk to cover and set aside for 5–10 minutes. Drain and proceed with the recipe.

Variation
For a more substantial version of tapenade, add 100 g/3½ oz drained canned tuna with the other ingredients. You may need to increase the quantity of oil. Add the extra oil in tablespoons at a time, blending after each addition until you achieve the required consistency.

WHITE SAUCES

Basic white sauce may be served completely plain or form the basis for an entire family of flavoured sauces, some of which are listed here.

🍽 Makes 300 ml/10 fl oz

🥄 Preparation time: 10 minutes, plus 20 minutes' standing (Béchamel Sauce)

🍲 Cooking time: 8–12 minutes

Ingredients

Basic White Sauce

25 g/1 oz butter, melted

25 g/1 oz plain flour

300 ml/10 fl oz milk

salt and pepper

Béchamel Sauce

300 ml/10 fl oz milk

1 slice onion

1 bay leaf

1 mace blade

5 black peppercorns

25 g/1 oz butter, melted

25 g/1 oz plain flour

salt and pepper

Cheese Sauce

25 g/1 oz butter, melted

25 g/1 oz plain flour

300 ml/10 fl oz milk

85 g/3 oz Cheddar cheese, grated

cayenne pepper

salt and white pepper

Parsley Sauce

2 –3 fresh parsley sprigs

25 g/1 oz butter, melted

25 g/1 oz plain flour

300 ml/10 fl oz milk

pinch of freshly grated nutmeg

salt and pepper

1 For the **Basic White Sauce**, put the butter, flour and milk into the blender and process until smooth. Pour into a saucepan and bring to the boil over a low heat, stirring constantly. Boil, stirring constantly, for 3–4 minutes until thickened and smooth. Remove from the heat and season to taste with salt and pepper.

2 For the **Béchamel Sauce**, pour the milk into a saucepan and add the onion, bay leaf, mace blade and peppercorns. Heat gently to simmering point, then remove the pan from the heat and set aside for 20 minutes to infuse. Strain the milk into the blender, add the butter and flour and process until smooth. Pour into a saucepan and bring to the boil over a low heat, stirring constantly. Continue to boil, stirring constantly, for 3–4 minutes until thickened and smooth. Remove from the heat and season to taste with salt and pepper.

Cook's tip
To prevent a skin forming on the surface of a sauce, place a layer of dampened greaseproof paper directly on the surface so that the sauce sticks to it.

3 For the **Cheese Sauce**, put the butter, flour and milk into the blender and process until smooth. Pour into a saucepan and bring to the boil over a low heat, stirring constantly. Continue to boil, stirring constantly, for 3–4 minutes until thickened and smooth. Remove from the heat, stir in the grated cheese until melted, then season to taste with cayenne pepper, salt and white pepper.

4 For the **Parsley Sauce**, blanch the parsley sprigs in a saucepan of boiling water for 30 seconds. Drain, refresh under cold water, then strip off the leaves and chop finely. Put the butter, flour and milk into the blender and process until smooth. Pour into a saucepan and bring to the boil over a low heat, stirring constantly. Continue to boil, stirring constantly, for 3–4 minutes until thickened and smooth. Remove from the heat, stir in the parsley and season to taste with nutmeg, salt and pepper.

HOLLANDAISE SAUCE

A favourite with poached asparagus and essential for making eggs Benedict, Hollandaise is also the basis for a family of sauces.

Makes about 175 ml/6 fl oz
Preparation time: 10 minutes
Cooking time: 10 minutes (Béarnaise Sauce)

Ingredients

Basic Hollandaise Sauce	Béarnaise Sauce	Mousseline Sauce
3 egg yolks	5 tbsp white wine vinegar	3 egg yolks
1 tbsp lemon juice	2 shallots, finely chopped	1 tbsp lemon juice
1 tbsp warm water	1½ tbsp chopped fresh tarragon	1 tbsp warm water
115 g/4 oz unsalted butter, melted	1 fresh thyme sprig	115 g/4 oz unsalted butter, melted
salt and pepper	½ bay leaf	salt and pepper
	3 egg yolks	125 ml/4 fl oz double cream, stiffly whipped
	1 tbsp warm water	
	115 g/4 oz unsalted butter, melted	
	salt and pepper	

1 For the **Basic Hollandaise Sauce**, put the egg yolks, lemon juice and water into the blender and process on low speed very briefly to mix. With the motor running, gradually add the melted butter through the hole in the lid. Continue to process until the sauce is thickened. Do not over-process or it will curdle. Transfer to a bowl and season to taste with salt and pepper.

2 For the **Béarnaise Sauce**, pour the vinegar into a small saucepan and add the shallots, 1 tablespoon of the tarragon, the thyme and the bay leaf. Bring to the boil and continue to boil until reduced to 1 tablespoon. Strain into a bowl and leave to cool. Put the egg yolks, cooled vinegar reduction and water into the blender and process on low speed very briefly. With the motor running, gradually add the melted butter through the hole in the lid. Continue to process until the sauce is thickened. Do not over-process or it will curdle. Transfer to a bowl. Stir in the remaining tarragon and season to taste with salt and pepper.

3 For the **Mousseline Sauce**, put the egg yolks, lemon juice and water into the blender and process on low speed very briefly to mix. With the motor running, gradually add the melted butter through the hole in the lid. Continue to process until the sauce is thickened. Do not over-process or it will curdle. Transfer to a bowl and season to taste with salt and pepper. Using a rubber spatula, gently fold in the whipped cream.

ASPARAGUS SAUCE

*This old-fashioned sauce has a delicate flavour and is an attractive colour.
It is delicious with plainly cooked poultry or fish.*

Makes about 300 ml/10 fl oz

Preparation time: 15 minutes

Cooking time: 25 minutes

Ingredients

150 ml/5 fl oz chicken stock

1 bouquet garni, consisting of 3 fresh parsley
   sprigs, 2 fresh thyme sprigs, 1 bay leaf and a
   small celery stick tied together

2 mushrooms, chopped

6 spring onions, chopped

700 g/1 lb 9 oz green asparagus

40 g/1 1/2 oz butter

4 tbsp chopped fresh parsley

2 tbsp plain flour

1 tbsp caster sugar

salt and pepper

1 Put the chicken stock into a saucepan and add the bouquet garni, mushrooms and 2 of the spring onions. Bring to the boil, then lower the heat, cover and simmer gently for 20 minutes.

2 Meanwhile, trim off and discard the woody ends of the asparagus stems. Blanch in lightly salted boiling water for 2 minutes, then drain and refresh under cold water. Drain well again.

3 Melt 25 g/1 oz of the butter in a heavy-based frying pan over a medium heat. Add the asparagus, parsley and remaining spring onions and cook, stirring gently, for 5 minutes. Remove from the heat.

4 Using a fork, mash the remaining butter with the flour to a paste to make beurre manié. Remove and discard the bouquet garni from the chicken stock. Stir in the beurre manié in small pieces at a time until they are absorbed and the mixture is thickened. Remove from the heat and leave to cool slightly.

5 Transfer the asparagus mixture to the blender and add the sugar. Add 4 tablespoons of the chicken stock mixture and season with salt and pepper. Process to a smooth purée, adding chicken stock mixture until you achieve the desired consistency. Stop and scrape down the sides as necessary. Taste and adjust the seasoning, adding more sugar, salt and pepper as required (the sauce should be quite sweet).

Variation
*For a simpler version of this sauce, omit step 1 and don't
bother to add the extra flavours to the chicken stock, but do
thicken it as in step 4. If the final sauce lacks colour, you
can add a few drops of green liquid food colouring.*

SATAY SAUCE

The mainstay of all barbecues, this sauce is great with kebabs, grilled pork or chicken and also goes well with salads such as Indonesian gado-gado.

Makes about 225 ml/8 fl oz
Preparation time: 10 minutes
Cooking time: 5 minutes

Ingredients

4 spring onions, coarsely chopped

1 garlic clove, coarsely chopped

2 tsp chopped fresh root ginger

6 tbsp peanut butter

1 tsp muscovado sugar

1 tsp Thai fish sauce

2 tbsp soy sauce

1 tbsp chilli or Tabasco sauce

1 tsp lemon juice

salt

coarsely crushed peanuts, to garnish

1 Put all the ingredients, except the crushed peanuts, into the blender. Add 150 ml/5 fl oz water and process to a purée.

2 Transfer to a saucepan, season to taste with salt and heat gently, stirring occasionally. Transfer to a bowl and sprinkle with the crushed peanuts. Serve warm or cold.

Cook's tip
You can use smooth or crunchy peanut butter. However, if you use sweetened peanut butter, omit the sugar. If the sauce is too thick, stir in a little canned coconut milk and reheat gently.

Variation
For a more authentic flavour, substitute tamarind for the lemon juice. Soak 1 teaspoon tamarind pulp in 3 tablespoons warm water, then press through a strainer into a bowl. You could also add 1 chopped lemon grass stalk to the sauce in step 1.

SLIM-LINE SALAD DRESSING

When you're watching your waistline, it's no good serving salads and then smothering them in high-calorie dressings, so here's a good alternative.

 Serves 4

 Preparation time: 5 minutes

 Cooking time: 0 minutes

Ingredients

Basic Slim-Line Salad Dressing

300 ml/10 fl oz natural
  low-fat yogurt

1 tsp English mustard

2–3 tbsp lemon juice

4 tsp sunflower oil

salt and pepper

Curry Dressing

300 ml/10 fl oz natural
  low-fat yogurt

2 tsp curry paste

2–3 tbsp red wine vinegar

4 tsp sunflower oil

salt and pepper

Green Dressing

300 ml/10 fl oz natural
  low-fat yogurt

2 tsp Dijon mustard

2–3 tbsp white wine vinegar

4 tsp sunflower oil

2 tbsp coarsely chopped
  fresh parsley

2 tbsp coarsely snipped
  fresh chives

2 tbsp coarsely chopped
  fresh tarragon

1 coarsely chopped spring onion

1 tbsp coarsely chopped
  watercress

salt and pepper

1 To make the **Basic Slim-Line Salad Dressing**, put all the ingredients into the blender and season to taste with salt and pepper. Process on medium speed until thoroughly combined.

2 To make the **Curry Dressing**, put all the ingredients into the blender and season to taste with salt and pepper. Process on medium speed until thoroughly combined.

3 To make the **Green Dressing**, put the yogurt, mustard, vinegar and oil into the blender and season to taste with salt and pepper. Process on medium speed until thoroughly combined. Add the parsley, chives, tarragon, spring onion and watercress and process for a few seconds to chop finely and blend.

Cook's tip

If the Slim-Line Salad Dressing or the Curry Dressing is thicker than you like, stir in 3–4 tablespoons of skimmed milk at the end. If you want to dilute the Green Dressing, add the milk and process briefly before adding the herbs.

FRUIT COULIS

*You can make a delicious sauce from most soft fruits to
go with ice cream, mousses and other desserts.*

🍽 Makes about 300 ml/10 fl oz

🥄 Preparation time: 5–10 minutes, plus 1 hour's chilling

🧤 Cooking time: 0 minutes

Ingredients

Peach Coulis	Melba Sauce	Tropical Fruit Coulis
450 g/1 lb peaches	450 g/1 lb raspberries, fresh	1 mango
1 tbsp lemon juice	or frozen	1 papaya
2 tbsp caster sugar	1 tbsp lemon juice	3 kiwi fruit
2 tbsp Amaretto liqueur	3 tbsp caster sugar	2 tbsp caster sugar
		3 tbsp white rum

1 To make the **Peach Coulis**, using a sharp knife, cut a cross in the base of each peach, then plunge into boiling water for 15–30 seconds. Drain and refresh in iced water. Peel off the skins, halve the peaches and remove the stones, then slice coarsely. Put the peaches, lemon juice and sugar into the blender. Process to a smooth purée, scraping down the sides as necessary. Transfer to a bowl and stir in the liqueur. Cover and chill for 1 hour.

2 It is not necessary to thaw frozen raspberries for **Melba Sauce**. Put the fruit, lemon juice and sugar into the blender. Process to a smooth purée, scraping down the sides as necessary, then rub through a sieve into a bowl to remove the pips. Cover and chill for 1 hour.

3 For the **Tropical Fruit Coulis**, cut the mango lengthways on either side of the large flat stone. Cut a criss-cross pattern in the flesh of the 2 slices without cutting through the skin. Turn inside out so the flesh resembles a hedgehog and slice it off the skin. Cut any remaining flesh away from the stone and put it all into the blender. Cut the papaya in half lengthways and scoop out the seeds with a spoon. Scoop out any fibres. Discard the seeds and fibres. Either cut or scoop the flesh, chop coarsely and add to the blender. Slice the kiwis and add to the blender with the sugar. Process to a purée, scraping down the sides as necessary, then rub through a sieve into a bowl. Stir in the rum. Cover and chill for 1 hour.

Cook's tip
*If you are serving these coulis to children, substitute
peach nectar for the Amaretto and orange juice
for the rum.*

CUSTARD

Custard is something of a family favourite and this group of recipes includes confectioner's custard for flan fillings and chocolate sauce.

◎ Makes 600 ml/1 pint (Custard); 300 ml/10 fl oz (Confectioner's Custard and Easy Chocolate Sauce)

🥄 Preparation time: 5 minutes

🧤 Cooking time: 5 minutes

Ingredients

Custard	Confectioner's Custard	Easy Chocolate Sauce
25 g/1 oz cornflour	55 g/2 oz sugar	115 g/4 oz plain chocolate, broken into pieces
600 ml/1 pint milk	2 eggs	
55 g/2 oz sugar	4 tbsp plain flour	150 ml/5 fl oz single cream
25 g/1 oz unsalted butter	½ tsp vanilla essence	225 g/8 oz caster sugar
1 egg	300 ml/10 fl oz milk	½ teaspoon rum essence
½ tsp vanilla essence	15 g/½ oz unsalted butter	(optional)

1 To make the **Custard**, put the cornflour into a bowl with 3 tablespoons of the milk. Stir to a paste. Put the remaining milk in a saucepan and bring just to the boil. Meanwhile, put the sugar, butter, egg and vanilla essence into the blender and process until smooth. Pour the hot milk into the cornflour mixture, stirring constantly. Return to the pan and cook over a low heat, stirring constantly, for 2 minutes or until thickened. With the blender motor running, pour the hot cornflour mixture into the blender.

2 To make the **Confectioner's Custard**, put the sugar, eggs, flour, vanilla essence and milk into the blender and process until smooth. Pour into a saucepan and bring to simmering point, stirring constantly. Cook, stirring, until thick. Remove from the heat and stir in the butter. Set aside to cool before using.

3 To make the **Chocolate Sauce**, put half the chocolate into the blender and process to chop, then add the remainder and process again. Pour the cream into a small saucepan and bring just to simmering point. Add the cream, sugar and rum essence, if using, and process until smooth.

Cook's tip

Keep the custard or sauce warm in a bain marie or heatproof bowl set over a saucepan of gently simmering water. Whisk occasionally.

CHAPTER 3: PURÉES AND DIPS

TARAMASALATA

*This popular Greek dip was originally made from smoked grey mullet roe,
but this can be difficult to get, so this recipe uses smoked cod's roe.*

Serves 6

Preparation time: 15 minutes

Cooking time: 0 minutes

Ingredients

2 slices white bread, crusts removed

5 tbsp milk

225 g/8 oz smoked cod's roe

2 garlic cloves, coarsely chopped

150 ml/5 fl oz olive oil

2 tbsp lemon juice

2 tbsp natural Greek-style yogurt

pepper

black olives, to garnish

1 Tear the bread into pieces and place in a shallow bowl. Add the milk and set aside to soak. Meanwhile, using a sharp knife, scrape the cod's roe away from the outer skin.

2 Tip the bread and milk into the blender and process until smooth. Add the cod's roe and garlic and process again. With the motor running, gradually pour in the olive oil through the hole in the lid. Process until smooth and with the consistency of mayonnaise.

3 Add the lemon juice and yogurt and season with pepper. Process very briefly to mix, then scrape into a bowl. Cover with clingfilm and chill in the refrigerator until required. Garnish with black olives to serve.

Cook's tip
Taramasalata is best made with quite a light-tasting olive oil, so don't use one from the Greek mainland, as these tend to be quite aggressive. Cretan or even French oils are lighter.

HUMMUS

This popular Middle-Eastern dip, made with chickpeas and tahini (sesame seed paste) is also good with salads and lamb chops.

Serves 6

Preparation time: 10 minutes

Cooking time: 0 minutes

Ingredients

225 g/8 oz cooked or drained canned
    chickpeas

150 ml/5 fl oz tahini, well stirred

150 ml/5 fl oz olive oil, plus extra to serve

2 garlic cloves, coarsely chopped

6 tbsp lemon juice

1 tbsp chopped fresh mint

salt and pepper

1 tsp paprika

1 Put the chickpeas, tahini, olive oil and 150 ml/5 fl oz water into the blender and process briefly. Add the garlic, lemon juice and mint and process until smooth.

2 Check the consistency of the hummus and, if it is too thick, add 1 tablespoon water and process again. Continue adding water, 1 tablespoon at a time, until the right consistency is achieved. Hummus should have a thick, coating consistency. Season with salt and pepper.

3 Spoon the hummus into a serving dish. Make a shallow hollow in the top and drizzle with 2–3 tablespoons olive oil. Cover with clingfilm and chill until required. To serve, dust lightly with paprika.

Cook's tip
To cook dried chickpeas, soak 175 g/6 oz dried chickpeas in cold water overnight. Drain, place in a saucepan and add cold water to cover. Bring to the boil, then lower the heat and cook for 2–2½ hours until tender. Drain well and leave to cool.

Variation
Strictly speaking, this dip is called hummus bi tahini. You can also make plain hummus by omitting the sesame seed paste if you find the flavour too intense.

SMOKED TROUT PÂTÉ

The delicate flavour and colour of smoked trout makes it the perfect choice when entertaining – and it's not expensive either.

 Serves 4

 Preparation time: 15 minutes, plus 1 hour's chilling

 Cooking time: 0 minutes

Ingredients

4 smoked trout fillets, about 200 g/7 oz each

115 g/4 oz cottage cheese

150 ml/5 fl oz crème fraîche

2 tbsp lemon juice

salt and pepper

lemon twists and fresh chervil
  sprigs, to garnish

rye or brown bread and butter, to serve

1 Skin the fish fillets and flake the flesh. Place the fish in the blender. Add the cottage cheese, crème fraîche and lemon juice and season with salt and pepper to taste.

2 Process until smooth, scraping down the sides as necessary. Spoon the pâté into 4 ramekins and smooth the surface. Cover with clingfilm and chill in the refrigerator for at least 1 hour.

3 To serve, uncover the ramekins and garnish each with a small twist of lemon and a sprig of chervil. Serve the pâté with slices of rye or brown bread and butter.

Variation
You could also make this pâté with other hot-smoked fish, such as mackerel or kippers. It would also work well with smoked monkfish, but this is very expensive.

INSTANT STORE-CUPBOARD PÂTÉ

This cheap and cheerful pâté is very popular with children and is a good way to encourage them to eat some healthy oily fish.

|◎| Serves 6
Preparation time: 10 minutes
Cooking time: 0 minutes

Ingredients

250 g/9 oz sardines in oil, drained
225 g/8 oz curd cheese
2 tbsp tomato ketchup

1 tbsp lemon juice
salt and pepper
lemon slice, to serve (optional)

1 Split open the sardines with a knife and remove and discard the back bones. Scrape off and discard the skin. It doesn't matter if the flesh breaks up.

2 Put the sardines, cheese, ketchup and lemon juice into the blender and process until smooth. Season to taste with salt and pepper.

3 Spoon into a serving dish, cover with clingfilm and keep in the refrigerator until required. Remove from the refrigerator 30 minutes before serving as this pâté tastes best at room temperature. Garnish with a slice of lemon if you like.

Cook's tip
Children will enjoy eating this with raw vegetables such as carrot batons, little celery sticks, whole cherry tomatoes and cucumber batons. It also goes well with oatcakes.

Variation
You can use virtually any canned, oily fish, such as mackerel or tuna instead of sardines.

CHICKEN LIVER PÂTÉ

This creamy pâté is extremely quick and easy to make and is ideal for serving with Melba toast as a dinner party starter.

Serves 6

Preparation time: 15 minutes, plus cooling, and 2 hours' chilling

Cooking time: 5–8 minutes

Ingredients

225 g/8 oz chicken livers

140 g/5 oz butter

2 garlic cloves, coarsely chopped

2 tsp chopped fresh sage leaves

2 tbsp Marsala wine

150 ml/5 fl oz double cream

salt and pepper

To garnish

55 g/2 oz butter

4–6 fresh sage leaves

1 Trim the chicken livers and chop coarsely. Melt 55 g/2 oz of the butter in a heavy-based frying pan. Add the chicken livers and cook over a medium heat for 5–8 minutes until browned all over but still pink inside. Remove the pan from the heat.

2 Transfer the chicken livers, in small batches, to the blender and process. Return all the livers to the blender and add the garlic, sage leaves and remaining butter. Season with salt and pepper.

3 Pour the Marsala into the frying pan and stir with a wooden spoon, scraping up any sediment, then add the mixture to the blender. Process until the pâté is smooth and thoroughly mixed. Add the cream and process again to mix. Spoon the pâté into individual pots and leave to cool completely.

4 Melt the butter for the garnish in a small saucepan over a low heat. Remove the pan from the heat and pour the melted butter over the surface of the cooled pâté. Arrange the sage leaves on top. Leave to cool, then cover with clingfilm and chill for at least 1 hour.

Cook's tip

To make Melba toast, lightly toast both sides of white bread slices until golden. Remove to a board and cut off the crusts. Using a long bread knife, slice horizontally through each slice to make 2 slices. Toast the uncooked sides until golden, then cut into triangles.

Variation

You can substitute either sweet or dry sherry, whichever you prefer, for the Marsala.

GUACAMOLE

Using the blender ensures that this is a very smooth version of the spicy Mexican dip. It's great with tortilla chips and also goes well with grilled steak.

Serves 6

Preparation time: 10 minutes

Cooking time: 0 minutes

Ingredients

juice of 1 lime

3 avocados

2 garlic cloves, chopped

3 spring onions, chopped

2 fresh green chillies, deseeded and chopped

2 tbsp olive oil

1 tbsp soured cream

salt

cayenne pepper, to garnish

1 Put the lime juice into the blender. Halve the avocados and remove the stones. Scoop out the avocado flesh with a spoon straight into the blender.

2 Add the garlic, spring onions, chillies, olive oil and soured cream and season with salt. Process until smooth. Taste and adjust the seasoning with more salt or lime juice.

3 Spoon the guacamole into a serving dish. Dust lightly with cayenne pepper and serve immediately.

Cook's tip

If you are making this in advance, delay adding the garnish. Cover the dish tightly with clingfilm and keep in the refrigerator for up to 2 hours. Stir, then garnish and serve. After 2 hours, the dip will begin to discolour.

Variation

For an unusual dip based on guacamole, put 1 tbsp lemon juice, 250 g/9 oz chopped cooked beetroot, 2 chopped garlic cloves, 25 g/1 oz fresh white breadcrumbs, 3 tbsp olive oil, and 2 tbsp creamed horseradish into the blender. Process until smooth and season with salt and pepper.

RED PEPPER DIP

This eye-catching, colourful dip is a good addition to a party buffet table and tastes great with a selection of crisp raw vegetables.

○ Serves 6

Preparation time: 10 minutes, plus cooling

Cooking time: 10–15 minutes

Ingredients

2 red peppers, halved and deseeded

2 garlic cloves

1 tbsp olive oil

1 tbsp lemon juice

25 g/1 oz fresh white breadcrumbs

salt and pepper

1 Place the pepper halves and garlic in a saucepan and add just enough water to cover. Bring to the boil, then lower the heat, cover and simmer gently for 10–15 minutes until softened and tender. Drain and set aside to cool.

2 Coarsely chop the pepper halves and garlic and place in the blender with the olive oil and lemon juice. Process to a smooth purée.

3 Add the breadcrumbs and process briefly until just combined. Season to taste with salt and pepper. Transfer to a serving bowl, cover with clingfilm and chill in the refrigerator until required.

Cook's tip
Don't forget that the quickest and easiest way to make breadcrumbs is in the blender.

Variation
You could also make this dip with orange or yellow peppers. Green peppers are not really suitable as they are rather acidic.

PEANUT BUTTER

Popular for sandwiches and snacks, peanut butter is also a useful ingredient when baking biscuits and, of course, for Satay Sauce (see page 42).

 Makes about 225 g/8 oz

Preparation time: 5 minutes

cooking time: 0 minutes

Ingredients

Smooth Peanut Butter

225 g/8 oz salted peanuts

3 tbsp groundnut oil

Crunchy Peanut Butter

225 g/8 oz salted peanuts

3 tbsp groundnut oil

1 For **Smooth Peanut Butter**, put the peanuts into the blender and process to chop them. With the motor running, gradually add the oil through the hole in the lid. Spoon into a screw-top jar and store in the refrigerator.

2 For **Crunchy Peanut Butter**, put the peanuts into the blender and process to chop coarsely. Remove 8 tablespoons of the chopped nuts and set aside. With the motor running, gradually add the oil to the blender through the hole in the lid. Spoon the mixture into a bowl and stir in the chopped nuts, then transfer to a screw-top jar and store in the refrigerator.

Variation
Other nut butters are literally made with butter. Blanch 115 g/4 oz nuts in boiling water for 1 minute, then drain and rinse in cold water. Place in the blender with 1 tablespoon cold water and process to a purée. Beat the purée into 225 g/8 oz softened unsalted butter.

BABA GHANOUSH

This popular Middle-Eastern dip has a wonderfully creamy consistency and is great served simply with warm pitta bread.

Serves 6

Preparation time: 15 minutes, plus cooling

Cooking time: 1 hour

Ingredients

2 large aubergines

1 garlic clove, chopped

2 tsp ground cumin

4 tbsp tahini

2 tbsp lemon juice

4 tbsp natural yogurt

2 tbsp chopped fresh coriander, plus
   extra to garnish

1 Preheat the oven to 220°C/425°F/Gas Mark 7. Prick the aubergine skins and place them on a baking sheet. Bake for 1 hour, or until very soft. Remove from the oven and set aside to cool.

2 Peel off and discard the aubergine skins. Coarsely chop the flesh and place in the blender. Add the garlic, cumin, tahini, lemon juice, yogurt and coriander and process until smooth and combined, scraping down the sides as necessary.

3 Transfer to a serving dish, sprinkle with a little coriander and serve. If you are cooking ahead, cover the dish tightly with clingfilm and store in the refrigerator until 30 minutes before serving.

Cook's tip
For a really authentic flavour, grill the aubergines over a barbecue to give them a smoky taste.

CHILLI PINEAPPLE DIP

You can make this dip as spicy or as mild as you like – its unusual flavour will certainly be a talking point among your guests.

Serves 6

Preparation time: 10 minutes

Cooking time: 10 minutes

Ingredients

2 tbsp olive oil

2 onions, chopped

225 g/8 oz fresh pineapple, chopped

½–1 tsp chilli powder

1 tsp ground cinnamon

1 tbsp white wine vinegar

salt

1 Heat the oil in a heavy-based frying pan. Add the onions and pineapple and cook over a low heat, stirring occasionally, for 10 minutes, or until golden.

2 Using a slotted spoon, and draining off as much oil as possible, transfer the onion and pineapple mixture to the blender. Add chilli powder to taste, the cinnamon and vinegar and season to taste with salt. Process until smooth.

3 Transfer to a serving dish, cover tightly with clingfilm and chill in the refrigerator until required.

Variation
You can also use canned pineapple. Drain well before chopping. Cook the onions for 5 minutes before adding the pineapple to the pan.

CHAPTER 4: SMOOTHIES AND DRINKS

MELON MEDLEY

Both watermelons and cantaloupes are among the most thirst-quenching fruits in the world and are perfect for summer drinks.

 Serves 4
 Preparation time: 10 minutes
 Cooking time: 0 minutes

Ingredients

Ginger Whizz

1 cantaloupe melon, halved and deseeded
4-cm/1 1/2-inch piece fresh root ginger, chopped
2 tbsp chopped fresh mint
chilled ginger ale or sparkling mineral water, to top up

Melon & Mango Tango

1 cantaloupe melon, halved and deseeded
600 ml/1 pint mango juice
2 tbsp fresh orange juice

Wild Watermelon

1/2 watermelon
300 ml/10 fl oz vodka

Watermelon Sunset

1 watermelon, halved
6 tbsp fresh ruby grapefruit juice
6 tbsp fresh orange juice
dash of lime juice

1 To make the **Ginger Whizz**, scoop out the melon flesh with a spoon straight into the blender. Add the ginger and mint and process until smooth. Pour into chilled glasses, top up with ginger ale or sparkling mineral water to taste, stir and serve.

2 To make the **Melon & Mango Tango**, scoop out the melon flesh with a spoon straight into the blender. Add the mango and orange juices and process until smooth. Pour into chilled glasses and serve.

3 To make the **Wild Watermelon**, deseed the melon if you were unable to find a seedless one. Scoop the flesh into the blender and process to a purée. Pour into a jug and stir in the vodka. Pour into chilled glasses and serve.

4 To make the **Watermelon Sunset**, deseed the melon if you were unable to find a seedless one. Scoop the flesh into the blender and add the grapefruit juice, orange juice and a dash of lime juice. Process until smooth, then pour into chilled glasses and serve.

Cook's tip
You can add ice cubes to the drinks to cool them, although this will dilute them. It is better to chill the ingredients and glasses first.

FRUIT FANTASY

Fruity drinks provide a great pick-me-up at any time of day and are
perfect for giving an energy boost first thing in the morning.

⦿ Serves 4
Preparation time: 10 minutes
Cooking time: 0 minutes

Ingredients

Fruit Kefir

1 banana

115 g/4 oz strawberries,
   halved

225 ml/8 fl oz peach yogurt

2 tbsp clear honey

225 ml/8 fl oz apple juice,
   chilled

Breakfast Bar

400 g/14 oz canned
   grapefruit and orange
   segments

4 tbsp lemon juice

3 tbsp lime juice

425 ml/15 fl oz orange
   juice, chilled

Perky Pineapple

handful of cracked ice

2 bananas

225 ml/8 fl oz pineapple
   juice, chilled

125 ml/4 fl oz lime juice

1 To make the **Fruit Kefir**, peel the banana and slice it directly into the
blender. Add the strawberries, yogurt and honey and process until smooth.
With the motor running, pour in the apple juice through the hole in the lid.
Pour into chilled glasses and serve.

2 To make the **Breakfast Bar**, tip the canned fruit and the can juices into the
blender. Add the lemon, lime and orange juice and process until smooth. Pour
into chilled glasses and serve.

3 To make the **Perky Pineapple**, put the cracked ice into the blender. Peel
the bananas and slice directly into the blender. Add the pineapple and lime
juice and process until smooth. Pour into chilled glasses and serve.

Cook's tip
If you can't find a can of mixed grapefruit and orange
segments, then substitute canned pink grapefruit.

MOCHA SHOCKER

Coffee and chocolate are two of the most popular flavours for drinks and they also make a superb combination.

Serves: 2
Preparation time: 10 minutes
Cooking time: 0 minutes

Ingredients

Mocha Flip-Flop
300 ml/10 fl oz strong black
    coffee, chilled
125 ml/4 fl oz milk
2 tbsp chocolate ice cream

Mocha Slush
handful of cracked ice
125 ml/4 fl oz coffee syrup
50 ml/2 fl oz chocolate syrup
225 ml/8 fl oz chilled milk
chocolate curls, to decorate

Super Mocha Slush
handful of cracked ice
125 ml/4 fl oz Kahlúa
50 ml/2 fl oz crème de cacao
225 ml/8 fl oz single cream
grated chocolate, to decorate

1 To make the **Mocha Flip-Flop**, put the coffee, milk and ice cream into the blender. Process for 1 minute, then pour into chilled glasses and serve.

2 To make the **Mocha Slush**, put the ice into the blender and pour in the coffee syrup, the chocolate syrup and the milk. Process until slushy. Pour into chilled glasses, decorate with chocolate curls and serve.

3 To make the **Super Mocha Slush**, put the ice into the blender and pour in the Kahlúa, crème de cacao and single cream. Process until slushy. Pour into chilled glasses, decorate with grated chocolate and serve.

Cook's tip
To crack ice, wrap ice cubes in a clean tea towel, gather up the corners to make a bag and bang the ice hard against a wall several times.

SODA FOUNTAIN

Fortunately, you don't need a hefty piece of machinery to make your own ice cream sodas and drinks – just a blender.

 Serves 1
 Preparation time: 5 minutes
 Cooking time: 0 minutes

Ingredients

Simple Soda

1 tbsp vanilla ice cream

2 canned peach halves, drained
  and coarsely chopped

4 tbsp single cream

150 ml/5 fl oz soda water,
  chilled

Typically Tropical

1 papaya

1 tbsp coconut ice cream

2 tbsp lime juice

150 ml/5 fl oz soda water,
  chilled

Tutti Frutti

1 tbsp strawberry ice cream

½ banana

½ pear, peeled, cored and
  chopped

4 tbsp milk

150 ml/5 fl oz soda water,
  chilled

1 To make the **Simple Soda**, put the ice cream, peach halves, cream and soda water into the blender. Process for 1–2 minutes, pour into a chilled glass and serve.

2 To make the **Typically Tropical**, halve the papaya lengthways and scoop out all the seeds (they are very peppery). Scoop out the flesh directly into the blender and add the ice cream, lime juice and soda water. Process for 1–2 minutes, then pour into a chilled glass and serve.

3 To make the **Tutti Frutti**, put the ice cream into the blender. Peel and slice the banana directly into the blender and add the pear, milk and soda water. Process for 1–2 minutes, pour into a chilled glass and serve.

BRILLIANT BERRIES

Soft fruits make wonderfully colourful and tasty drinks. This is a great way to encourage your children to eat more fruit.

🍽 Serves 4
🥄 Preparation time: 5 minutes
♥ Cooking time: 0 minutes

Ingredients

Merry Berry
large handful of crushed ice
450 g/1 lb strawberries
125 ml/4 fl oz grenadine
ginger ale, to top up

Cool Cranberries
350 g/12 oz cranberries,
   thawed if frozen
425 ml/15 fl oz cranberry
   juice, chilled
300 ml/10 fl oz natural yogurt
2–3 tbsp clear honey

Strawberry Colada
450 g/1 lb strawberries
125 ml/4 fl oz coconut cream
600 ml/1 pint pineapple juice,
   chilled

1 To make the **Merry Berry**, put the crushed ice into the blender. Reserve 4 strawberries for decoration and put the remainder into the blender with the grenadine. Process until smooth, then pour into chilled glasses and top up with ginger ale. Decorate each glass with a strawberry and serve.

2 To make the **Cool Cranberries**, place the berries and juice in the blender and process until smooth. Add the yogurt and the honey and process again until combined. Taste and add more honey if necessary. Pour into chilled glasses and serve.

3 To make the **Strawberry Colada**, reserve 4 strawberries to decorate. Halve the remainder and place in the blender. Add the coconut cream and pineapple juice and process until smooth, then pour into chilled glasses, decorate with the reserved strawberries and serve.

Variation
You can substitute your favourite berries in any of these recipes – raspberries for strawberries (remember that they have seeds) or blackberries for cranberries, for example.

Going Nuts

Nuts are little powerhouses of energy, so these drinks and smoothies are quick ways to restore get-up-and-go whenever you're beginning to flag.

 Serves 2

 Preparation time: 10 minutes

 Cooking time: 30–60 seconds (Almond Milk and Double A)

Ingredients

Almond Milk	Choconut Special	Double A
25 g/1 oz blanched almonds	2 bananas	25 g/1 oz blanched almonds
300 ml/10 fl oz milk, chilled	4 tbsp smooth peanut butter	225 g/8 oz canned apricot
125 ml/4 fl oz natural yogurt	2 scoops chocolate ice cream	halves in natural juice
2 tbsp caster sugar	300 ml/10 fl oz chilled milk	150 ml/5 fl oz apricot yogurt
	chopped peanuts, to decorate	$1/4$ tsp ground cloves

1 To make the **Almond Milk**, dry-fry the almonds in a heavy-based frying pan, tossing and turning frequently, for 30–60 seconds until golden. Remove from the heat and leave to cool, then place in the blender and process until finely chopped. Add the milk, yogurt and sugar and process until smooth. Pour into chilled glasses and serve.

2 To make the **Choconut Special**, peel and slice the banana directly into the blender. Add the peanut butter, ice cream and milk and process until combined. Pour into chilled glasses, decorate with a sprinkling of chopped peanuts and serve with a straw.

3 To make the **Double A**, dry-fry the almonds in a heavy-based frying pan, tossing and turning frequently, for 30–60 seconds until golden. Remove from the heat and leave to cool, then place in the blender and process until finely chopped. Drain the apricots, reserving half the can juice. Coarsely chop the apricots and add to the blender with the reserved juice. Process briefly, add the yogurt and cloves and process again until smooth. Pour into chilled glasses and serve.

Cook's tip
Always check nuts for freshness before using – while they are a very useful store-cupboard ingredient, they can go off if kept for too long.

Five a Day

People often overlook vegetables as ingredients for drinks and smoothies, but lots of them are really fabulous.

◎ Serves 2
🥄 Preparation time: 10 minutes
🧤 Cooking time: 0 minutes

Ingredients

24 Carrot

handful of cracked ice
2 carrots, coarsely chopped
115 g/4 oz canned pineapple
   pieces in juice, drained
175 ml/6 fl oz pineapple
   juice, chilled
cucumber slices, to decorate

In the Pink

1 blood orange
5-cm/2-in piece of cucumber,
   peeled and cut into chunks
300 ml/10 fl oz tomato juice,
   chilled
dash of Worcestershire sauce
salt
cucumber slices, to decorate

On the Beet

175 g/6 oz cooked beetroot,
   chopped
125 ml/4 fl oz orange juice,
   chilled
5 tbsp natural yogurt, chilled
150 ml/5 fl oz still mineral
   water, chilled
salt
orange slices, to decorate

1 To make the **24 Carrot**, put the ice into the blender, add the carrots, pineapple pieces and pineapple juice and process until slushy. Pour into chilled glasses, decorate with cucumber slices and serve with straws.

2 To make the **In the Pink**, peel the orange, removing all traces of white pith. Holding it over a plate to catch the juice, cut out the segments from the membranes. Squeeze the membranes over the plate to extract any juice. Place the segments and the juice in the blender. Add the cucumber and tomato juice and season to taste with Worcestershire sauce and salt. Process at high speed, then strain into chilled glasses and serve, decorated with cucumber slices.

3 To make the **On the Beet**, put the beetroot, orange juice, yogurt and water into the blender and season to taste with salt. Process until smooth, then pour into chilled glasses and serve, decorated with orange slices.

Cook's tip
Cooked beetroot is well known for staining hands and fingers – you could wear protective gloves while handling it to avoid this.

CHAPTER 5: DESSERTS

EASY ORANGE CHEESECAKE

*Everyone's favourite, cheesecake is a melt-in-the-mouth dessert
or a special treat served with morning coffee.*

Serves 6

Preparation time: 25 minutes, plus 2 hours' chilling

Cooking time: 5 minutes

Ingredients

115 g/4 oz digestive biscuits

55 g/2 oz butter, plus extra for greasing

225 g/8 oz curd cheese

150 ml/5 fl oz natural yogurt

½ packet orange jelly (100–115 g/
   3½–4 oz), torn into cubes

1 tbsp sugar

grated rind and juice of 1 orange

200 g/7 oz canned mandarin
   orange segments, drained

1 Break up the biscuits and process in batches in the blender to make crumbs. Melt the butter in a small saucepan over a low heat. Remove the pan from the heat and stir in the biscuit crumbs. Lightly grease a 20-cm/8-in loose-based flan tin, then press the buttery crumbs into it. Place in the refrigerator to chill until the crust has set.

2 Meanwhile, place the curd cheese and yogurt in the clean blender and process to combine.

3 Heat 3–4 tablespoons water in a small saucepan, then remove from the heat and add the jelly. Stir until dissolved, then stir in the sugar and the orange rind and juice. Add the mixture to the blender and process until smooth. Pour the filling into the biscuit crumb case and chill in the refrigerator for 2 hours, or until set.

4 Carefully remove the cheesecake from the tin and place on a serving plate. Arrange the mandarin segments around the edge of the cheesecake and serve.

Variation
*This cheesecake also tastes wonderful and looks
lovely decorated with fresh raspberries.*

CHOCOLATE ICE CREAM

Home-made ice cream is a real treat with its rich texture and delicious

flavours, and chocolate has to be the number one flavour.

🍽 Serves 4

🥄 Preparation time: 30 minutes, plus cooling and freezing

🧤 Cooking time: 15–20 minutes

Ingredients

1 vanilla pod

850 ml/1½ pints milk

115 g/4 oz plain chocolate, broken into pieces

4 egg yolks

115 g/4 oz caster sugar

300 ml/10 fl oz double cream

salt

1 Slit the vanilla pod lengthways and place in a saucepan with the milk. Bring just to simmering point, then remove from the heat and set aside. Place the chocolate in a heatproof bowl and set over a saucepan of barely simmering water, stirring occasionally, until melted. Do not allow the base of the bowl to touch the surface of the water. When the chocolate has melted, remove from the heat and set aside to cool completely.

2 Remove the vanilla pod and stir the chocolate into the milk. Put the egg yolks and sugar into the blender, pour in the chocolate milk and add a pinch of salt. Process until thoroughly mixed. Pour the mixture into a heatproof bowl set over a saucepan of barely simmering water and cook, stirring constantly, until the custard has thickened and will coat the back of a spoon. Remove from the heat and leave to cool.

3 Whisk the cream until softly peaking, then fold it into the cooled chocolate custard. Pour the custard into a freezer-proof container, cover and place in the freezer for 1 hour, or until ice crystals have formed around the edges. Scoop the ice cream into the blender and process until smooth. Return to the container and place the container in the freezer for 1 hour.

4 Process the ice cream in the blender again, then return to the freezer. Repeat this process once more then freeze until firm. Transfer the container to the refrigerator 15 minutes before serving to allow the ice cream to soften slightly.

Cook's tip
If you have a hand-held blender you can use this to beat the semi-frozen ice cream without removing it from the freezer-proof container.

Variation
To make coffee ice cream, substitute 2 tablespoons instant coffee granules for the vanilla pod, stirring until they have dissolved. Omit the chocolate. Alternatively, don't omit the chocolate and make mocha ice cream.

PEACH FOOL

This family favourite is easy to make. Although fools are traditionally made with 'sour' fruit, such as gooseberries and rhubarb, peaches are scrumptious.

⊙ Serves 4

Preparation time: 10 minutes, plus 2 hours' chilling

Cooking time: 0 minutes

Ingredients

225 g/8 oz peaches

1 quantity Confectioner's Custard (see page 48)

150 ml/5 fl oz double cream

amaretti, to serve

1 Using a sharp knife, cut a cross in the base of each peach, then plunge into boiling water for 15–30 seconds. Drain and refresh in iced water. Peel off the skins, halve the peaches and remove the stones, then slice coarsely.

2 Put the peaches into the blender and process to a smooth purée. Mix the purée into the confectioner's custard until thoroughly combined.

3 Whisk the cream until stiff, then fold it into the custard mixture in 2 batches. Divide among serving dishes or glasses and chill in the refrigerator for at least 2 hours. Serve with amaretti.

Variation
For rhubarb fool, chop 250 g/9 oz rhubarb into chunks and place in a saucepan with 25 g/1 oz caster sugar and 1 tablespoon water. Cover and simmer gently for 10–15 minutes, until softened. Drain and process to a purée and combine with the confectioner's custard.

STRAWBERRY ICE

A simple fruit-flavoured 'water' ice is one of the most refreshing desserts imaginable at the end of an al fresco lunch on a hot summer's day.

Serves 4

Preparation time: 15 minutes, plus freezing

Cooking time: 0 minutes

Ingredients

500 g/1 lb 2 oz strawberries, hulled

100 g/3½ oz caster sugar

125 ml/4 fl oz orange juice

1 tbsp lemon juice

1 Place the strawberries, sugar, orange and lemon juice in the blender and process until smooth and the sugar has dissolved completely. Taste and add more sugar and/or lemon juice.

2 Pour the mixture into a freezer-proof container, cover and place in the freezer for 1 hour, or until ice crystals have formed around the edges. Scoop the ice into the blender and process until smooth. Return to the container and return the container to the freezer for 1 hour.

3 Process the ice in the blender again, then return to the freezer. Repeat this process once more then freeze until firm. Transfer the container to the refrigerator 10 minutes before serving to allow the ice to soften slightly.

Variation

Virtually all soft fruits make delicious ices, so try substituting the same quantity of raspberries or loganberries for the strawberries. Push the purée through a nylon sieve before freezing to remove the seeds.

MELTING MANGO DESSERT

Luscious mango and spicy ginger is a combination made in heaven and the perfect way to end any meal.

🍽 Serves 6

🥣 Preparation time: 15 minutes, plus 1 hour's chilling

🧤 Cooking time: 0 minutes

Ingredients

3 mangoes

3 pieces of stem ginger in syrup

3 tbsp stem ginger syrup

5 tbsp crème fraîche

3 egg whites

chopped almonds or pistachios, to decorate

1 Cut the mangoes lengthways on either side of the large flat stone. Cut a criss-cross pattern in the flesh of the 2 slices without cutting through the skin. Turn inside out so the flesh resembles a hedgehog and slice it off the skin. Cut any remaining flesh away from the stone and put it all into the blender.

2 Add the stem ginger, ginger syrup and crème fraîche and process until smooth. Scrape the purée into a large bowl.

3 Whisk the egg whites in a separate, grease-free bowl until they form soft peaks. Gently fold the egg whites into the mango purée with a rubber spatula. Divide the mixture among serving dishes, cover and chill in the refrigerator for at least 1 hour. Sprinkle with the chopped nuts before serving.

Cook's tip

Stem ginger in jars is widely available from supermarkets. It consists of young ginger shoots that have been cooked and preserved in a sugar syrup.

Variation

Substitute 3–4 large ripe bananas for the mangoes. Peel, then slice them directly into the blender.

KIWI SORBET

Sorbets are a little more substantial than water ice but not so rich as ice cream. They look great when made with colourful fruits such as kiwi.

Serves 6

Preparation time: 15 minutes, plus cooling and freezing

Cooking time: 5–8 minutes

Ingredients

700 g/1 lb 9 oz kiwi fruit

4 tbsp orange juice

140 g/5 oz caster sugar

strip of thinly pared lemon rind

1 To peel a kiwi, cut a thin slice off both ends, then stand it upright on a chopping board and slice off the remainder of the skin vertically in strips. Try not to remove too much of the flesh. Peel all the kiwis and cut into quarters. Place them in the blender with the orange juice and process to a purée.

2 Put the sugar and lemon rind in a heavy-based saucepan and pour in 175 ml/6 fl oz water. Bring to the boil, stirring until the sugar has dissolved, then remove the pan from the heat and set aside to cool.

3 Remove and discard the lemon rind from the sugar syrup. Stir in the kiwi fruit purée and mix well. Pour the mixture into a freezer-proof container, cover and place in the freezer for 1 hour until ice crystals have formed around the edges. Scoop the sorbet into the blender and process until smooth. Return to the container and replace the container in the freezer for 1 hour.

4 Process the sorbet in the blender again, then return to the freezer. Repeat this process once more then freeze until firm. Transfer the container to the refrigerator 10 minutes before serving to allow the sorbet to soften slightly.

Variation
Tropical fruits make colourful sorbets. You could substitute 1 large mango, stoned, peeled and chopped, for the kiwi fruit, or 700g/1 lb 9 oz papaya, peeled, seeded and chopped, for the kiwis and lime rind and juice for the lemon rind and orange juice.

ORANGE COEURS À LA CRÈME

These little heart-shaped moulds are perfect for Valentine's Day
or any time that you're feeling romantic.

Serves 4
Preparation time: 10 minutes, plus 6 hours' chilling
Cooking time: 0 minutes

225 g/8 oz ricotta cheese
225 g/8 oz mascarpone cheese
55 g/2 oz caster sugar
grated rind and juice of ½ large orange
Peach Coulis (see page 47), to serve

1 Put the ricotta cheese into a blender and process briefly until smooth. Add the mascarpone, sugar, orange rind and juice and process until combined.

2 Line 4 coeur à la crème moulds with muslin, then spoon the mixture into them. Smooth the surface and place the moulds on a flat plate or tray to catch any liquid that drains during setting. Place in the refrigerator and chill for 6 hours or until set.

3 To serve, turn the moulds out onto individual plates and surround with a pool of peach coulis.

Cook's tip
If you don't have any coeur à la crème moulds, spoon all the mixture into a muslin-lined sieve and set it over a bowl in the refrigerator for 6 hours. To serve, spoon the mixture into lightly greased ramekins, then turn out onto plates.

Variation
You can substitute curd cheese for the mascarpone and the rind and juice of 1 lemon for the orange rind and juice, if you like.

PANCAKES

These can be as simple or elaborate as you like. Children love them with syrup,
but you can also fill them with cream and fruit or even flambé them in liqueur.

🍽 Serves 4–6
🥄 Preparation time: 10 minutes, plus 15–30 minutes' standing
🧤 Cooking time: 12–15 minutes

Ingredients

2 eggs

425 ml/15 fl oz milk

175 g/6 oz plain flour, sifted

2 tsp caster sugar, plus extra for sprinkling

25 g/1 oz butter, melted

lemon wedges, to serve

1 Put the eggs and milk into the blender and process briefly to combine. With the motor running, gradually add the flour and sugar through the hole in the lid. Process until just combined and free of any lumps, but be careful not to over mix.

2 Pour the batter into a jug, cover and leave to stand for 15–30 minutes to allow the starch grains to soften and expand.

3 Heat a crêpe pan over a medium heat until it is very hot. Brush with melted butter. Stir the batter and pour 3–4 tablespoons into the pan. Tilt and rotate the pan to spread the batter evenly. Cook for 30–40 seconds until the pancake is set, the underside is lightly browned and the top has small holes in it. Shake the pan to loosen, then flip the pancake over with a palette knife or toss, if you prefer. Cook the second side for 30 seconds.

4 Slide the pancake onto a warm plate and keep warm while you cook the remainder, brushing the pan with more melted butter as required. Stack the pancakes interleaved with greaseproof paper until you are ready to serve.

5 To serve, roll or fold the pancakes and place on warm plates. Sprinkle with sugar and serve with lemon wedges for squeezing.

Cook's tip
To test whether the crêpe pan is hot enough, sprinkle a
couple of drops of water on the surface. If they sizzle
immediately, the pan is ready to use.

Variation
For savoury pancakes, simply omit the sugar from the
batter. They can be filled with cooked spinach and ricotta
cheese or ham and mushrooms and served with Cheese
Sauce (see page 36).

INDEX